उषा किरण द्वारा रचित
'जो रह गई थी अनकही'
का अंग्रेज़ी अनुवाद

What Remained Unsaid

Translated by
Dr. Shakuntala Prasad

SAMANT
PUBLISHING

ISBN : 9788199862500
Edition : First, March 2026
Title : What Remained Unsaid
Author : Usha Kiran
Translated by : Dr Shakuntala Prasad

Published by

SAMANT PUBLISHING

An Imprint of **Taneesha and Prachi NextGen Publication**

Registered Address: Plot No. 48, Khasra No. 646, Road No. 2,
Suman Nagar, Bahadarabad, Haridwar, Uttarakhand – 249402, India
Website : www.samantpublishing.com
E-mail : support@tpnextpub.com
Phone : +91 9760418103

Printed by :
Manipal Technologies Limited, Bengaluru - 560001, Karnataka

Lovingly dedicated to my grandchildren —

Dr Soumya Baxi, Parul, Rhea,

Tanya and Nikita.

- **By Shakuntala Prasad**

From the Author's Pen

It is said that words originate within the boundaries of a language. Nonetheless emotions can't have any restrictions. Dr Shakuntala Prasad, who is just like my elder sister, has efficiently and sincerely translated the emotions of my poems into English, maintaining the liveliness and spirit of the poems. Hence the translation is not just a technical collaboration for me but its creativity and the formative style is very close to my heart. She translates not only words but also the feelings and sensibilities. I admit it's not easy to render the depth of feelings into another language (here English) yet she has very efficiently preserved the soul of the words as if forming a bridge of emotions. This was impossible without her creative imaginations.

Infact she has given a world - wide recognition to my expressions.

Without her support, my book could hardly reach out to international readers. I am extremely grateful to her.

In the end, I want to say one more thing that it's a matter of immense pride for me that the preface of this book is written by Dr Varindra Kumar Varma Ji. He has been a teacher in Shantiniketan. Any praise about his accomplishments is like "showing a lantern to the sun."

My heartfelt thankfulness to dear Shakuntala Prasad Dii and Dr Varindra Kumar Varma Sir.

Usha Kiran
27th January 2026

A Note from Translator

Dear Readers,

It gives me great joy to present to you “Jo Reh Gayi Thi Ankahi (What Remained Unsaid)”, a translated collection of poems by Usha Kiran. This marks my second foray into translation, following “Rhythm of Life (Jeevan Ki Laya)”, which was also drawn from her deeply moving work.

I must confess, translation was never a path I had imagined for myself. My heart has always found comfort in crafting poems, stories, memoirs, and travelogues. But something changed when I began reading Usha Kiran’s poetry. Her words spoke to me in a way that was impossible to ignore—piercingly honest, exquisitely expressive, and profoundly human. I felt an overwhelming urge to share her voice with those who might not otherwise encounter it. That calling gave birth to this translation.

Usha Kiran is someone I have known since many years—more than a friend, she is like a sister to me. Knowing her personally, I have seen how her life has been marked by both struggle and strength. The grace with which she has transformed her lived experiences into poetry—honest, tender, and full of quiet resilience—is nothing short of inspiring. Her command over the Hindi language, her heartfelt style, and her ability to translate emotion into verse with such clarity are what compelled me to take on this labour of love.

Translating her poems has been both a challenge and a privilege. At times, I found myself pausing over certain words—terms like ‘sawan’ or ‘dhani churiyan’—which are rich with cultural nuance but nearly impossible to replicate in English without losing their soul. In such cases, I chose to retain the original words, trusting that their beauty and significance would still resonate, even in unfamiliar form.

I am reminded of a moment from my teaching years, when I came across Longfellow’s poetry rendered into Hindi by both Harivansh Rai Bachchan and Sumitranandan Pant. Both translations were masterful, yet not a single word overlapped. It was a powerful lesson—that translation is not mere substitution, but a reimagining. It demands empathy, intuition, and above all, fidelity to the feeling behind the words.

In that spirit, I offer this book to you—not just as a translation, but as a heartfelt effort to preserve and share the spirit of Usha Kiran's work. I hope it touches you, moves you, and stays with you as it has done for me.

Last but not the least, 'Preface' to "Jo Reh Gayi Thi Ankahi" is by Dr Varindra Kr Varma, a great poet, scholar and a prominent name in Hindi and English Literature. It's my privilege that inspite of his old age health issues, he could spare time to read my book and give his opinion. I am extremely grateful and thankful to him.

Your thoughts, feedback, and suggestions would mean a great deal to me. They will guide and inspire me as I continue on this unexpected but rewarding path.

With warmest regards and best wishes,

Shakuntala Prasad
UK
February 2026

प्रस्तावना
(Preface)

दिल की इबारत ही सच्ची कविता होती है। भाषा में अभिव्यक्ति का माध्यम गद्य भी है और पद्य भी और इन दोनों के बीच अंतर इसी बात को लेकर है कि एक में अभिव्यक्ति विचार प्रधान होती है तो दूसरे में भावना प्रधान। इसी बात को मोटे तौर पर ऐसा भी कह सकते हैं कि कविता अंतःस्फूर्त अभिव्यक्ति का नमूना है। अंतःस्फूर्त का अर्थ यह है कि वह दिल से निकली हुई भावाभिव्यक्ति है। इसका मतलब यह भी है कि जो कवि नहीं है, किसी मौके पर उसकी बोली हुई चीज़ भी कविता हो सकती है। इसका एक उदाहरण मैं यहां प्रस्तुत करना चाहूंगा। एक बार की बात है, बहुत साल पहले हम अपने परिवार के साथ इंदौर से खंडवा जा रहे थे। हमारी ट्रेन को पर्वत श्रेणियों के बीच से गुजरना था। शाम का समय था और सूरज ढलने का वक्त था। दो पहाड़ियों के बीच प्रकृति का अद्भुत दृश्य देखने को मिला। बड़े आकर का सूरज अपनी लालिमा लिए दो पर्वत श्रेणियों, जो आपस में एक दूसरे के बहुत नज़दीक थीं, उनके मध्य से ढलता हुआ दिखाई दिया। कहने का मतलब यह है कि वह पहाड़ियों के बीच से ऊपर से नीचे जाता हुआ दिख रहा था। वह दृश्य बहुत रमणीय था। और उसे देखकर मेरी छह साल की बच्ची इतनी उत्तेजित हो गई कि उसके मुख से अचानक यह शब्द निकल पड़े : "मम्मा...मम्मा देखो... देखो ना मम्मा... और भैया तुम भी देखो न... आसमान कैसे डाल रहा है... "पृथ्वी के गुल्लक में ...सोने का सिक्का" । बच्ची के मुख से खुशी के जो शब्द अनायास निकले वे उसके दिल को आनंदित करने वाले शब्द थे। प्राकृत सौंदर्य का यह दृश्य मेरी इस छोटी सी बच्ची को इतना अभिभूत कर गया कि उसके मुख से तात्कालिक रूप से जो शब्द निकलें वे कविता की तरह ही प्रतीत हुए। कहने का तात्पर्य यह है कि प्रकृति के उस दृश्य को देखकर उसकी शोभा का वर्णन बिना किसी विचार के जिन शब्द संयोजन के साथ हुआ, वह कविता ही तो थी। इसी बात को हम ऐसा भी कह सकते हैं कि बच्ची के मुख से एक कविता फूट निकली। "फूट निकली" शब्दों का मतलब यही है कि ऐसी अभिव्यक्ति अनायास थी और उसमें दिल के खुश होने की अभिव्यक्ति थी। इसी बात को हमने शुरू में इस तरह कहा था कि कविता दिल की इबारत होती है।

अधिकतर ऐसा भी देखा गया है कि जब बोलने वाला और सुनने वाला एक ही भाव भूमि पर होते हैं तो एक के मुख से निकली हुई भावाभिव्यक्ति दूसरे के मन में कविता का भाव जगा सकती है। भक्ति भाव में डूबे व्यक्तियों की सामूहिक अभिव्यक्ति भजन में रहकर कीर्तन में बदल

जाती है। लेकिन ऐसा भी होता है कि एक के द्वारा अभिव्यक्त भाव दूसरे में उसी भाव को जगा भी सकता है और ऐसी स्थिति भी काव्याभिव्यक्ति का उदाहरण हो जाती है। भक्ति भाव में डूबा व्यक्ति जब भगवान राम को बाल रूप में नया- नया चलने का अभ्यास करते हुए देखता है, तो उनके लड़खड़ाने को देखकर वह बहुत व्याकुल हो जाता है किन्तु उनके संभलने पर आनंदित होता है और इसी बात को वह अपनी कविता में कुछ इस तरह व्यक्त करता है, "ठुमक चलत ...रामचंद्र... बाजत पैजनिया" ... उस समय उसे इस बात का ध्यान नहीं रहता कि वे तो भगवान है, गिरने का क्या प्रश्न उठता है। लेकिन उसके मन में धुक धुकी रहती है कि कहीं बच्चा गिर न जाए। पर जब ऐसा लगता है कि बच्चा अब गिरा कि तब गिरा, वह अपने आप ही संभल जाता है और तब उसमें आश्वस्ति का भाव जग जाता है। इस प्रसंग में "ठुमक चलत रामचंद्र" को इस अंदाज में अगर कहा जाए कि "ठुमक ठुमक चलत राम" तो अभिव्यक्ति ज़्यादा सटीक एवं प्रभावशाली बन जाएगी। ' ठुमक' शब्द का दो बार इस्तेमाल किए जाने पर यह आभास देता है की छोटा से बच्चे ने जब पहला कदम रखा तो लड़खड़ाया लेकिन संभल गया। और उसी अंदाज में आगे भी बढ़ता रहा। तो बच्चे के चलने का यह अंदाज भय और आश्वस्ति के भाव को बनाए रखता है। कहने का तात्पर्य है यह है कि उसके चलने और गिरने के पहले खुद संभल जाने की स्थिति बड़ी मनभावन और सुखद लगती है। ' ठुमक' शब्द का प्रयोग अगर एक जगह की बजाय एक साथ दो बार किया जाए तो अभिव्यक्ति इसलिए भी आकर्षक हो जाती है क्योंकि बच्चे का डोलना और फिर गिरते गिरते संभल जाने का जो दृश्य है, वह एकदम साफ नज़र आता है।

इसीलिए मैंने प्रारंभ में कहा था कि कविता का आरंभ दिल से होता है। लेकिन अब यह भी कहना चाहूंगा कि उसका अंत बुद्धि के साथ होता है। दिल और दिमाग का जितना अच्छा सामंजस्य होगा उतनी अधिक अच्छी कविता होगी। कवि की प्रतिभा के मूल्यांकन में यह बात महत्वपूर्ण है कि उसमें जल्दबाज़ी न की जाए। भाव और विचार के ताल मेल को बैठाने में कोई कविता कितना वक्त लेगी, वह कवि के बस की बात नहीं होती। फिर भी सामंजस्य बनाए रखने के लिए कोशिश तो करनी होगी। अभी तक जो भी बातें कहीं गई वह प्रासंगिक उन लोगों के लिए हैं जो अपनी अपनी भाषा में कविता लिखते हैं। समस्या तब उठती है जब किसी एक भाषा की कविता का दूसरी भाषा में अनुवाद किया जाए। अनुवाद की समस्याएं ढेर सारी हैं। उनको जानने, समझने और जांचने की जरूरत है। कहने का मतलब यह है कि अनुवादक को उन दोनों भाषाओं का अच्छा ज्ञान हो और कविता के मर्म को दूसरी भाषा में उसी अंदाज में अभिव्यक्त करने की प्रतिभा हो।जब तक कि कोई दोनों भाषाओं के ज्ञान के साथ साथ शब्दावली एवं कविता के स्वरूप का ज्ञान नहीं रखेगा, कविता का अनुवाद उसके लिए बहुत कठिन होगा।

इस पुस्तक में उषा किरण की हिंदी भाषा में रचित कविताओं का अनुवाद डॉ. शकुंतला

प्रसाद ने अंग्रेजी भाषा में किया गया है। यहां ये बताना चाहूंगा कि कवयित्री उषा किरण बिहार की प्रसिद्ध कवियित्री हैं और इन्हें दो साल पहले यानी 2023 में कई सम्मान मिले हैं, जैसे काव्य कुसुम सम्मान, काव्य कलश सम्मान, रंगोत्सव सम्मान, नव सृजनकर सम्मान और स्वर प्रवाह। इन्होंने विविध विषयों पर हिंदी भाषा में अपनी कविताएं लिखी हैं जिनका अनुवाद डॉ.शकुन्तला प्रसाद ने अंग्रेजी भाषा में किया है। डॉ. शकुन्तला प्रसाद मेरे बड़े साले की पत्नी हैं और मैं इन्हें विगत 54 सालों से जान रहा हूं। इन्होंने अपनी स्नातकोत्तर एवं पी एच डी की उपाधि अंग्रेजी साहित्य में ली है। इनकी विशिष्ट रुचि हिंदी और अंग्रेजी साहित्य में शुरू ही से रही है और ये बीच - बीच में दोनों भाषाओं में कविता, लेख एवं लघुकथाएं भी लिखती रहीं हैं। इनकी रचनाएं विभिन्न पत्र - पत्रिकाओं में प्रकाशित भी हैं। चूंकि ये दोनों भाषाओं में समान रूप से ज्ञान और पकड़ रखती हैं और कविता के मर्म को भी समझती हैं, इसीलिए इन्होंने इतनी सहजता के साथ कविताएं अनूदित की ।

कवयित्री उषा किरण ने प्रस्तुत पुस्तक "जो रह गयी थी अनकही" लिखी है, इसका अनुवाद भी अंग्रेजी में शकुंतला प्रसाद ने ही किया है। आशा की जा सकती है कि इसके पहले की कविता संग्रह की तरह प्रस्तुत संग्रह की कविताएं और उनका अनुवाद भी पाठकों को पसंद आएगा और कवयित्री और अनुवादिका की जोड़ी आगे भी साथ साथ अपने साहित्य सेवा का सफर बराबर जारी रखेंगी। कवयित्री और अनुवादिका दोनों बधाई की पात्र हैं। मेरी शुभकामनाएं इनके साथ हैं।

डॉ. वारींद्र कुमार वर्मा

सेवानिवृत्त प्राचार्य (उच्च शिक्षा)1995.

हिंदी एवं अंग्रेजी भाषा के अंतर्राष्ट्रीय स्तर के प्रतिष्ठित साहित्यकार, समालोचक, भाषा विश्लेषक, व्याकरण विशेषज्ञ एवं अनुवादक।

फरवरी 2026

Acknowledgements

I wish to acknowledge with utmost gratitude -

Usha Kiran, just like my sister who inspired and encouraged me throughout.

My sons, daughters - in - law and my grandchildren, for their love, patience and forbearance - I feel truly blessed to have you as my children.

My wonderful siblings and wider family, especially my sisters for all their affection along the roller coaster of life.

My special friends and people I met along life's sojourn, whose love and friendship I will cherish forever.

Most importantly, my eldest son Neeraj and Rashmi for taking out time to read my work and advise. Last but not the least, Pammi was always there for me… without whose support, love and care, I could not do anything.

Shakuntala Prasad

February 2026

Index

Jo Reh Gai Thi Ankahi

Which Never Could Flow
(जो कभी बहे नहीं)

1 wonder
How long can one
Run away from memories?
Often one window closes
Another opens ....
Flowers preserved
In old books,
Drift us to bygone days;
The past becomes alive;
But deep down my heart,
A question always arises.
Where have the tears gone which could never flow???

The Two Words
(दो लब्ज)

Mornings
Drenched with dew - drops
Cosy warm sunny Noons,
Smiling lustrous Evenings,
Downpour of dreams at
Nights,
And….
Winter bidding goodbye…. whispers
The story of 'two words'
In my ears …
You being it's first word
As also the second one!!

None the less, now that
You are not here,
There is no story!!
This petty matter is
So easy to speak…. yet
Is so difficult to
Bear!
Alas!
If only you could
Understand this!!!!

Tracks
(पगडंडी)

Tracks -
Narrow, crooked … Uneven, muddy -
Impermanent -
Full of
Untrimmed wild
Grass and dry shrubs…
Along with pebbles n clods of earth;
Walking on it
One is reminded of his
'Existence'…
Also how
it teaches
That discomforts may be
Unpleasant —-
None-the-less, teach -
That Struggles,
Bring out courage and tolerance in you…
And make you dream
Of constructing TRACK
Which will take travellers
Towards the goal!!

The Knots
(वो गिरहें)

The silky phase of life —-
A bit complicated…
When
Love strikes ….
Two hearts beat together,
Everything
Seems soft, smooth, heavenly;
But
Everything changes!!!
If there is a knot therein
And
It’s never easy to open
And separate the tangled knots…
They hurt throughout life…
It’s not in control
Either to make knots
Or to open one!!!
That’s why
These tangled knots give
A lifetime of
Sharp stinging sensation!!!

What remained Unsaid
(जो रह गई थी अनकही)

The first image
On a blank paper,
Creates the most intense effect;
That's why
In the waves of memory
Desires come and go -
And repeatedly
Keep on stinging
The heart…
And
As time flies….
The unfulfilled wishes,
Slowly in the form of words …
Make us realise
That there were a lot of
Things that remained
UNSAID!!!!

Incomplete Painting
(अधूरा चित्र)

The Sudden showers
Mixed up the
Colours from the painting
On the canvas…
The picture was smudged —and
Remained only some
Faded blurred lines!!!
A question, abruptly
Flashed in my mind!
Life too, is similar -
We keep on filling it
With a variety of Different colours
-But suddenly
Call comes from the
Unseen Supreme Diety
And remains only the
Incomplete painting!!

Probably You Will Remember Me
(शायद याद आऊँ मैं)

When Golden rays
Of morning
Descending from the sky
Caress your face Smoothly -
Even if you don't wish,
Probably you'll
Remember me.

Amid scorching
Hush n rush of Life -
Some bitter n better memories
Stroke your heart …
Even if you wish to forget,
Probably
You'll remember me.

Whenever
In dark brown light of
Evening,
Breeze whispers
Love-notes in your ears,
Even if you don't wish to
Listen,
Probably
You 'll remember me.

In an intoxicating
Moonlit night;

Silvery glimmer of moon
Peeping in sea -
Trouble your heart -
Reminding you of
Someone's
Loving company…and
You become restless;
Even if you don't opt to Accept…
Probably
You'll remember me!!!

Keep Going
(चरैवेति चरैवेति)

Tales of bygone times
Are like waters of pond -
Stagnant…still
But Life, like a river, is
Always moving …
That's why -
Like a river,
Sometimes slow, sometimes fast …
At times stopping
Then taking a turn
Facing the challenges of life…silently patiently…
With strong faith
Ever hopefully
Moves ahead in Life
Only moving forward -
Chanting within…
Keep Going…. keep going!!

Charm
(कशिश)

Relationships of love
Are not all Roses and Jasmine;
Exist there
Some flower - beds
Which
Are barren…
With only thorns…
And are ever pricking!!
Yet, there's a charm in that
Thorn - prick too;
Which don't allow any Change in the face n Form of the relationship
And preserve the
Fragrance of that charm
All through their
Life!!!!

Your attraction
(तुम्हारा आकर्षण)

Sitting around fire
In severe cold,
Ash from fire
Flying upward -
Reddening of eyes -
Feel of your attraction
Every moment!!!

Feelings of your heart
Written on small piece of Paper…reading again n Again …getting lost in
Bygone days —-
Feel of your attraction
Every moment

Like carefree easterly breeze passing by the side
Saying nothing when Asked, convey
Something only through Eyes,
Feel of your attraction
Every moment!!!

Listening to you,
Without blinking eyes,
Gazing at you …
A sense of abrupt
Stopping of
Water from spring ….
Feel your attraction

Every moment!!!
Distanced from you
Learnt to live …
Yet, a feel of crackling
Of glass in between
Stones….
Feel of your attraction
Every moment!!!

Yes !!feel of your Attraction even today
Every moment!!!!

A Poem
(नज्म)

I agree
When you say that,
"Life is a battle";
But you hardly realise
That in this Battle,
The memories create
Deep pain, agonies and sufferings
While the gathering of
Memories keeps getting Decorated …
One keeps passing through them again n again….
In fact…
It's then that
A poem is born….
On a blank paper!!!

Provender
(पाथेय)

The
Moment I remember you,
Waves sprinkle conch shells on
Glimmering sandy beach;
Morning Sun - rays
Traverse through
Palm leaves.
Moon light at night
Glorify the shells -
As l pick them …
Taking your name;
I tie and keep the
Splendour of our
Sweet companionship -
In my dupatta -
As a token of the
Happy days we spent together!!
They are very precious!!!
Infact, these are
The alms of LOVE
Providing comfort...
As I move forward
On uneven tracks of
Life like a pro vender

Moon
(चाँद)

Yesterday night
The Sharad 'Full Moon'
Was showering upon Earth
It's silvery white dark yellowish glory ....

Drenched in its
Light shower, I was
Delicately arranging
Dreams in my eyes!!!
Wished to ask....
What is LOVE??
Is it only gazing lovingly
At each other??
OR
Being together
For the entire life???

True Love
(सच्चा प्यार)

LOVE is not a pebble
Thrown in calm waters
Of a pond …
Creating bubbles for a
While and then
All peaceful

LOVE is not a
Rainbow - popping up
After downpour,
For a while in the
Clear blue sky
Beautifying and alluring
Everyone for sometime
And then gone!!!

LOVE is not
A bird perched on the Parapet….
When aimed at by urchins, just flies away!!

True LOVE Is
Like NORTH STAR,
Ever shining
In a fixed direction
In the celestial sphere….
With an unending glow.

Spring the Name of Love
(बसंत एक प्यार का नाम)

Singing 'Bhairavi 'at dawn;
Listening to 'darbari '
During noon;
Humming 'malkauns' at nights….
All around a nameless smell floats….
And gradually a moist Voice conveys into the Ears that-
Spring is the name of Love!!
Just as love, it doesn't Visit constantly!!
That's why they say
"Jindagi pyar ki do char ghadi hoti hai…."

Musk Deer
(कस्तूरी मृग)

Without realising that we have been already
blessed with love and happiness-
We keep on praying for them…
Although
Life is somewhere around, we are
Wandering -
Searching for them
Here and there …
Like a musk deer.

Woman
(औरत)

If a woman gets a drop of love
She
can make it a rain - shower and
Drench herself therein.

She can sometimes,
Take it as a river -and
Swim therein.

She can even take that drop
To be a lake….and
Making a home on its bank, can
Decorate it with all her fancies, and
Start living there in.

Yes,
Woman does know
To cherish even the
Little things.
She knows how to handle things
And
Wants to maintain
All her relationships.

Loneliness
(तन्हाई)

Loneliness is
Like a piece of cloud
Wandering here n there
In the sky!!!
Like a tramp!!!

Loneliness sizzles
Somewhat
Like a lone fisherman
Feeling very hot
In the mid- sea!!!

Loneliness
Spreads like the waters
Of a huge dam that
Crumbles abruptly at once.

Flowers of Palash
(पलाश के फूल)

When the month of 'Magh' comes to an end -
Winter, in its old age, is Breathing its last…
Then
Spring season gradually
Attaining its adulthood knocks at the corner,
And with the arrival of "phalgun",
The Spring exuberantly
Covers the 'Palash Tree'
With deep orange red flowers... which look like
A parrot's beak.

It seems as if
"Palash Tree" is the chief
Guest of Nature's
Festival of "Phagua"!!

Your Letter
(तेरी चिट्ठी)

Whenever I open the
Engraved small brass box
Wherein l treasured
Your letters for years,
The scent, like those from
Flowers in garden;
Spreads through my Mind-
The faded yellow worn - out pages of the letters cherish all past
Sweet n sour memories…
Your finger - touch on them, like a rainbow -
Appears in front of my eyes….!!!!
A number of events flash
In my mind n heart…
So much so that
Scenery of
The present just disappears
And Past takes over the
Screen of heart n soul.

Poems
(कविता)

That can be felt -
During difficult times,
With smiling kids,
In a poet's heart,
In Nature,
In Lover,
In stones ….
As also in the
Eye moisture…
Which prevents Earth
From having cracks on its crust …
Or in warmth of palms,
Which stops world from once again
Returning to Ice age ….
Or heart 's beating - deep down,
Yet heard from distance ….
As also in -
All the emotions that
Inspire, give courage and strength…
That which is felt is
POEM.

Incomplete is Complete
(अधूरा ही मुकम्मल)

In the evening of life -
Moments of
Conversations … pass Through memory lane … When right from the
Beginning to the end -
Could never speak what really wished to say!

Perhaps there are a few Things, that when left Incomplete are
Complete!!

Circumstances
(हालात)

In the quietness of night
Your silence,
In my thoughts -
Screams in such a way that
Even if I feel drowsy …
No sleep is there.

During days full of noise,
The empty eyes
Speak out everything
About your face …
And circumstances
Are such that ….

They say,
Some persons
Look so good even
Though they are Broken!!

Passion
(जज़्बा)

Every extinguishing ‘Deeya’ wishes to light
A new ‘deeya’
Before it is doused.
As it is said that
Life is the name of
A brief journey …
That’s why
In any phase of life
The light of human
Passion should burn
Just like ‘Deeya’
Until…….
It is extinguished…!!

Spring At its Prime
(शबाब पर बसंत)

When
Cool, pleasant, soothing
Vasanti Breeze,
Begin to invigorate the Body….
When creepers which
Shrink in cold winter...
Begin to bloom and sway
In the festive Spring …
When -
Bees begin to hover over
Sweet tasting
Honey - drops In orchards;
And
Flowered mustard fields
All aglow with golden hues - under the blue sky;
Then understand that -
"Pushpdhanwa" - God of Beauty …has shot his
Five arrows;
And Spring has
manifested itself in full.
The Spring has arrived…
With flowers of Mango Tree, humming
'Saraswati Bandana '-
Swinging, strutting. wriggling….
Inviting 'Holi' with handfuls of green, yellow, red and pink
'Gulal'
…
Proudly acclaiming that
Spring is at its Prime.

Progress
(प्रगति)

Every house
Has a strange noise
Of absolute stillnes!!!
Silence is prospering!
Lips are shut!
Relationships distant!
Heart, although,
Wants to have
Intimate conversations
With relatives …
However,
Lost and forgotten
Are the effect Fragrance of those
Lovingness —
In the name of progress!

Spring - In Your Company
(बसंत के संग)

Bougainvillea Shines,
In the parapet,
New leaves glow …
On the swaying creeper;
Delicate branches tremble and
'Mahua' drops on the ground …
Do not aim with a catapult….
Mustard all yellow n radiant;
Like sunshine!!!
Enjoy the Glory of SPRING!!!
Breeze, pleasant,
Makes fun -
'Nag kesar' flowers-
Heavily laden
Blow beautifully like hair …
'Harshingar' orange n white, oozes out sweet
Fragrances all around …
The anklets n bangles of
New brides
Create pleasing sound —
Without hurting her wrists,
Slowly open the clasps; Her arms are ready to
Hug the Spring lovingly!!!
It's all with you
O Spring ….in your Company!!

Hunger
(भूख)

Two small palms Stretched before me -
Stroking lovingly, slowly
Took his soiled hands in Mine and pampering,
Pat his shoulders…
His face remained the Same, no change of Expression was there…
Without even blinking -
His eyes just stared at
Me…hands spread as Before, remained cold
And chill….
Finally I placed some Coins on them and
Suddenly his wide open Eyes shone bright with
Joy and Hope …
True,
Love alone doesn't
Satisfy HUNGER!!!

Relationships
(रिश्ते)

Relationships are like
Old locks …
If not opened for long
It rusts
No key would open it Then …finally
It must be broken.

A trace of light
(क़तरा आलोक का)

A sense of emptiness
Creeps into my heart -
Creating an unknown Pain …unaware am I
How and why it happens.
My mind just boggles
Frequently….
As if a broken- winged Bird within me, is Impatient to soar up in the sky ...
But then from a remote corner of fate,
A storm is raised,
And a strange pain
Sets into my heart!
Yet, in this dust - storm
Within my heart
Still remains a small trace of light.
Which
Always pushes me ahead like a pillar of light.

This is the light of love…
of remembrance.

Relations
(संबंध)

With time, the meanings
Of relations have changed a lot.
Earlier, like a plant, any relation was nurtured by
Closeness, intimacy between people ….
Whereas of late
Everywhere there are
Strained relationships,
A lot of discrepancies
And inconsistencies!!
And
There are times
When the delicate
Situations force
To accept n tolerate the
Most adverse reactions
Like a 'Neel kanth'

Today's Era
(आज का दौर)

In the modern era
'Home' seldom exists…
There are' houses ', where
Exist cracks of hatred on walls…
Ego seeps through
The roof…
Silence, like music,
Rings in every home.
And
The people who live -
Instead of cleaning
The algae and seepage-
Take shelter in separate Rooms, to keep themselves safe n secure….
With wraps of silence
Around them!!!

Speak up Basant
(बोल बसंत)

To welcome 'Basant'
Dawns a state of lntoxication on Earth!
With slow speed of a swan
Slowly, in a rhythmic
Pace, Earth decorates herself -
Sun- rays write love -Letters on shining drops
Of dew!
Cuckoo's melodious Voice excites so that
Heart- beats sing
Something quietly…
Gust of wind blows …
And it's very difficult
To keep control on self.
Sun-rays, like a sackful
Of turmeric, caress Bodies on Earth...
The partner of 'Kamdeo', Rati, infuses
Love into material and Conscious …
Red - pink,yellow- green
Spread simple golden
Scents…
Without being touched
Each pore of body is aroused …
Gleefully blooms….
Every moment becomes Festive as if with dance and
Melodious musicals …
In such a scenario
We become one with
Nature …. Can anyone

Stay unaffected?
Isn't that truthful and Captivating??
Speak up Basant!!
Speak up Basant!!!

In Holi
(होली में)

Intoxicate from inside
The beating of
Drums and cymbals;
Create a stir
In Holi every day!!

Happy and excited
As a young beautiful
Woman…
No regrets no remorse
No grief
In Holi every day!!

Open the lip- lock
Read the letter of Weather…. Even the
Dumb will speak….
In Holi everyday!!

Do not question
The state of mind…
The branch is loaded
From within
Inebriated, petrichor,
Delicious….
In Holi everyday!!

Colourful looks
Like flying shadows

Clouds all ‘gulal’
In Holi everyday!!

Water guns full of
Colored water
In hand… Krishna
Compels Radha to play
In Holi everyday day!!

Plant Trees Save Earth
(वृक्ष लगाओ धरा बचाओ)

Nature's unique creation
Is TREE
It's the most beautiful gift….
Branches all decorated
Green green leaves
Give shelter to birds
Through them
Life rejoices, sings,Sways …
Bearing heat and cold
Enjoys the gifts of
Basant….
Taking in the 'drig jal'
Of Earth…
Gives out drops through
The leaves
Always keen for charity
Least interested in
Taking n grabbing …
Trees teach the ways
Of life
They realise the Dreams.
Never tired of 'giving '
What belongs to them -They just spend n Giveaway their gifts …
We know only to receive
Never learnt to give back
Life is meaningless
Without trees
As rainy season is useless without clouds

We have never seen Heaven…
Have only woven dreams
Having forgotten the
Benefits of trees
Have invited the Disasters for us

That's why we say
Plant Trees and Save
Earth.

Difference
(अंतर)

'Par' (in Hindi) having
Two meanings, is so Small a word ...
With the meaning' wing'
It gives life to a tiny bird.
With wings it soars high
In the vast expanse of he Sky...
The other meaning is 'But'.... states confusion-
Forcing one to stay Where he was...
This is the difference-
One inspires to fly high
Up towards the sky....
The other embodies
Grievances and regrets!!

Thinking
(सोच)

Man has drawn many
Criss- cross lines
On our beautiful Earth
Revolving in space…
Wherever the lines meet
Man stands with his
Mind and soul ….
Be it the changing dates
Of calendar or
Rotation of the Greenwich clock…
Dates become history…
And
Looking at burning lamp
On Tulsi platform,
Will we be left behind
The times?
Or will we be moved out of the world?
If tying ties and flying on
Flying cots, will we be
The first citizen of World??

That Manjar
(वो मंजर)

Without you, anyhow
I learnt to live
But couldn't learn
To be happy!
And now have even forgotten —-
What the issue was!!!!

Had even made a lot of
Vows
And tied 'many wish - threads"
But perhaps could not tie the thread between
Two hearts...
Yet, have still left
One Breath for
The 'manjar' when,
At the junction of
Love n Existence,
You yourself will say
That whole life has been
Washed off….
Cleaning the memories
From life.

How to Forget
(कैसे भूलें)

I wish to
Cry so much at one go
That
The flowing tears
May wash away
His picture
Imprinted in my heart!
But
My eyes keep waiting
With hope n desire
Fondly caressing
And kissing
Every fragment of his
Memory in my heart …
How can l ever
Forget him at all?

Storm of Emotions
(जज़्बात के तूफ़ान)

At times man thinks -
What if the
Boat did not reach
The shore ……
At least the
Storm has subsided ….
But it's his mistake!
Many a time man
Saves his life…
Yet his soul
Remains stuck
In that
Storm of emotions!!!

Clouds of Aashadh
(आषाढ़ी घटा)

O! The clouds of Aashadh!!
Your first rain drops
Not only remind of
'Megh doot';
But the aroma arising
From the wet Earth....
When immortal Nectar like drops of rain fall...
They
Wake up so many
Memories that had
Been sleeping ....!!!

Indeed, O clouds of
Aashadh!!
Your pouring rain drops
Not only soak
Earth with water
But also submerge -
Man in the
Memories residing in
The middle- aged lines
Of his forehead.

Silence
(खामोशी)

I wonder how
Life, Moment and Time
Entangle with each other
In their own way;
None- the- less,
Although having
A stock, full of words,
You never could say
One simple Sentence
Comprising of a few words!!
I, however, kept quiet;
Apprehending, if you
Would refuse,
I'll not be able to breathe!!
And amid this confusion
The silence stayed on
Between both of us Forever!!!

Mother
(माँ)

'Mother' is- not just a Calling word ...
It's a complete world!
For a child, inspite of his Best efforts, it's impossible to describe
Her in words ....
Dictionaries
Fall short of words to define her.

Even after she passes Away, the loving Fragrance of Her love n
affection -
Tied in each weave
Of her 'Anchal'-
Permeates every corner of home....

That's why even after
Her demise,
She is never gone!!!
Truly,
Mother is forever
With her children -
In form of Prayers!!!

This Heart
(यह दिल)

We think
Human being is very Strong…. He can tolerate
All turmoils and troubles
Of life!
But there are times
When
He is not strong, but
Helpless …every
Storm crosses through Him ….
He has No choice.
But to bear it!
How obstinate and
Powerless
Is this heart!!!
Even the blow of reality
Cannot improve it.

Time
(समय)

It's good
Time never stops!
Otherwise,
All wounds would be
Ever fresh…
Dry dead tree
Would be standing
Forever!

Time doesn't recognise
Own or outsiders…
It only knows
How strong is it!!!

Maiden Love
(काचा प्यार)

Still fresh in my mind
Is that Holi -
When all of a sudden
Avoiding everyone's gaze, you appeared
In front of me
And smeared me with colours.
All wet was I -
Head to toe…
Speechless l stood …
In fear…. what will they say?
Childish n innocent me!!!
Years passed by —
Since then,
Many a time was wet with colours - but
No more timid n simple
Was I.
However
Never experienced again
That amazing feeling ….
Of the whole being drenched with colours….
Perhaps, because
That was an exquisite Sensation of pure raw Love's
Permanent colour.

Memories Should Be with Us
(यादों का बने रहना)

When life is
At cross - roads,
I delve into the
Golden moments
Of my memory;
Stored carefully,
Like a precious treasure,
In the depth of my heart;
Therein
I get all my answers,
All solutions. .....
True, in Life,
It's important that
Memories should
Always be with us.

Love
(प्रेम)

Love
Has no date:
Comes secretly
And
In mute language of Eyes,
Gives meaning to the
Life- long prayers of each other …
Then with an intoxicated
Sensation our hidden
Charm is fertilised …
Thus, love
In a simple way…
Instinctively, for a few
Moments, locks the
Four eyes in an
Unblinking gaze!!

Weapons
(हथियार)

EntireWeapons are
Not used in Battles only!!
Some of them are
Used in a very silent way
And we don't even realise,
When it's
Poisoned sharp edges
Have stirred and even Wounded our soul.

Fragrance of Spoken Words
(बातों की खुशबू)

Fragrances are of
Different kinds!
Pleasing smell of
Flowers ….
Of Perfumes …
Which
fade away after a limit.
But the
Real fragrance, Swaying
Like an evergreen creeper,
With its sweet charm,
Oozes out from such words
Which,
Even after they are spoken and they are
Finished …
Their sweet smell
Remain with us
For the whole life!!!!

Incomplete Tale
(अधूरी दास्ताँ)

Feelings of naive age are
More dangerous
Than angry waves of Sea; And
When the Windows of
Noise of those waves
Open, a number of
Incomplete tales -
Like fresh gusts of wind,
Shake our minds and soul.

You
(तुम)

You said
You will count the
Days for my return …
I thought you will say
That you will count
Minutes, seconds, every
Moment ….
You said to look for road...
While I felt you would ask
Me to accompany you …
Effortlessly,
All those moments Passed -
The mood of the time Changed
You were now a pain
Which couldn't be Treated ….
And then the words were
All lost in accepting
The reality!!!

Free Will
(अपनी मर्जी)

Heart if cut into a
Hundred pieces …
And rendered lifeless -
Even then -
A portion of it is certainly
Alive where resides it's Free will…
There it wishes to live
It's own Dreams!!
But generally Circumstances and Fate
Don't allow it to inhibit …
Yet it is always in the Lookout for a chance-
When the God above May Bless and give him
A pen, so that he
May write his fate
Himself.

Importance of Relationships
(रिश्ते की अहमियत)

How much importance
The person in front of
You, gives you - is
Evident from his Mannerisms ….
Actually the mannerism
Has a language of its
Own….
There is, however, no
Scale to measure
The love in relationships.
Because -
The heart, itself,
Is a scale…
Wherein all the readings
Show up automatically…
Your's as also of
Others.

How to Address
(क्या संबोधन दूँ)

In the morning
As I see theSun-rays
At Dawn,
A question flashes in
My mind …how
Should I address her?
Shall l call her
Dinkar's beloved,
Bride Or something Else

During golden mornings
Like Dinkar's beloved …
She, sometimes hides,
At times smiles….
And radiates the red glow all around.

Then Sun gradually
Adorns her, with its divine light, putting
Vermillion on her hair - partition…and
Makes-her his bride.

But as soon as she
Becomes bride,
At dusk
The bride melts
And vanishes
In the dusky evening.

Desires
(ख्वाहिश)

Desires should have
Boundaries!
If left independent
And free -
Man is left with no Values;
But ……if
Desires remain unfulfilled and
Turn Into yearning,
Even then,
There is regret
In the Heart!!!!

Noise
(शोर)

Noise is created
Not only by sound;
But
Sometimes by
Silence as well.
And
Noise created by
Silence, has more weight.
It leaves the person
Speechless and
Internally shaken.

Love- Conversations
(प्रेम - संवाद)

Unlimited is the stock of
Words ....
Never get tangled up
In its measurement and weightage....
You
Speak something,
Without moving your lips -
And l will listen,
Without lowering my eye-lids ...always Remember one thing
That
Conversations of love
Are never dependent
On words!!!

Debt of Relationship
(रिश्ते का क़र्ज़)

A life is still waiting
At that very turn of life -
Where she was standing
Yesterday -
Expecting someone ...
To pay him back the debt of Relationship.
If only there could be
A borderline -
To pay off the
Debt of Relationships.

Agony
(पीड़ा)

In the Mornings
Blooming Amaltaas;
Blossoming Rose Mary;
Slipping of Katahri Champa ….
But the
Loneliness of day - time
Blends with heaviness
Of evenings;
And
Waves of varied feelings
Getting moulded
Into words n relationships -
Always remind me of
That betrayal of yours
That's why
Each blurry evening -
Agony of my open eyes,
Solidifies across the
Horizon!!!

Ability to Live
(जीने का सामर्थ्य)

At times
If you get hurt
By something…
That pain
Instantly takes you
Through ages!!
But the solid ground of realities
Of life,
Shatter the dreams….
Afterwards, he pain that Follows;
Comes in your fist
Like a magic …
Becoming your
STRENGTH!!!!
This indeed, is the
REALITY OF LIFE!!!

Calculations
(हिसाब किताब)

Strange are the
Tick - tock of the Needles of a clock!
It's not only difficult
But impossible to
Calculate its moves!!
Completely confusing!!
With each tick - tick,
AGE advances,
And … and
With the same tick - tick
Life gets shorter.!!!

Remembered You
(तुम्हें याद किया)

Whenever I remembered you,
Spring stood at my closed door….
Knocking at the door -latch n humming;
I opened the closed door;
And offered all my
Childish, playful Gestures
To that spring season!!!

Memory
(स्मृति)

In the speed against time
We tend to forget
A lot of things …
Against that forgetting,
Pushing it behind,
Memory boldly stands up.

In fact
There is no life without memory.
And, without
An alert life ……
There is no memory!!!

Daughter
(बेटी)

Till the time
Daughter is a kid,
Her laughter says a lot; An idol of tenderness and love;
She fills hearts -
Embracing her own daughter,
Tries to weave her Incomplete dreams;
Clinging on to the aanchal of mother …
She flows like
A bubbling stream.
Kneading damp lump of clay …. she shapes out things …runs all over
The wet mossy slippery
Grounds of courtyard,
Without slippers
Touching ground just runs n slips
Enlightened Mum simply
Enjoys
Whenever she sings
Melodiously… strolling
around she
Swaggers
Like a Doll,
With her tinkling silver anklets!!!
But when
Daughter herself Becomes a Mother!!
She fills everything
While herself remains
Empty …
She keeps away the sorrows of the family!!

Safeguards
From grief, distress and misery;
Workship and Time
She balances!!!!

Infact victorious
Kalpana and Sushmita, Pratibha Patil or
Draupadi Murmu
Are all
The exemplary
Daughters!!!
Making the Universal flag fly
High!!!

Existence of Father
(पिता का अस्तित्व)

The everyday busy life
Moving on a rough trail
Tired n exhausted—
Father is the cool
Breeze eliminating that
Smell of sweat!!

After rains
In the clear blue sky
Peeping through cluster
Of flowers like the varied colours of Rainbow …
Is the Existence of Father!!

Around fire
In a shivering night
The golden rays of
Morning sunshine falling
On the cold - shrunk faces…This is
Father's existence!

On hilly slopes
On leaves of green
Trees …like the shining
Sunlight on lingering
Dew -drops, is the
Existence of Father!!

Truly, only Father

Is the base of our first
Introduction,,,,,
He is the warrior
In whose shelter we are
Always safe!!!
That's why
Eternal is the
Existence of Father!!!

Same as Before
(जस का तस)

There was much truth
In what you said …
The sorrows of those
Left behind are greater
Than those who move
Forward …
Your remark with
Innocent laughter -
Rings in my ears for a Long time!!
Do you remember that
Moment??
Infact!! Even today I
Hear that echo -
Same as before!!!

Picture
(तस्वीर)

Today, with a brush in
Hand, created cross- wise colours ...of the
Tempest in my mind...
Of life's hot desert
Of tired depressed
Footsteps ...
Of deserted lanes of
Dreams...
Of the fragrance of your memory ...
Of intellectual infinite
Love- soaked cool calm
Eyes...
Of entangled silky threads...
Which remained somewhat untouched,
Unsaid, unsolved ...
And ....
As I looked at canvas...
Was amazed to see that
I had made your picture
On the blank canvas.

Door Latch
(दरवाज़े की कुंडी)

Everyday
When strings of heart
Ring with chirping of birds …
Ring quite deliberately
The swaying leaves of
Trees….
The red yellow green
Glass bangles of
Full wrists ring…
Ring the musical anklets
With every step ….
Ring the gamuts of
Golden dreams in
Sleep….

So many things ring…
But never rings
The door - latch.

Love: A Sensation
(प्रेम: एक अहसास)

The fling opening of
Windows- doors —
At once is
The profound sensation of Love!!
Where all differences of
'You' and 'I' get
Eliminated…
Just as, in the battlefield
Lahana Singh took the gun- shot on his chest
To save "her" husband…well exhibiting his deep
Satisfaction in keeping
The memory of that
'Small meeting' with her long ago - alive
In his memory …
Hence
The story,
'Usne Kaha Tha '
Is the fiercest guard
Of the sensation of
Love!!!

Date
(तारीख़)

Past is not a piece of
Paper with something
Written on it….
Which can be torn and
Thrown out as per wish…
It can visit anytime
And knock at your closed
Doors- sometimes wrapped in a pink shawl
Or, in scorching noon…

And date is just
A mirror of time!!

Scent of Books
(किताबों की खुशबू)

Many things changed
As age advanced …
One thing that never
Changed is my fancy for
Books!
Peeping and prying
Through new and old books …
Conversing and enjoying the noiselessness of
Book shelf ….
Words speaking
Even talking
Especially old books like old friends … their
Smell intoxicating,
Reigning supreme…
Take you in a different
World …….
There is peace, Inebriation and a
Solace of mind n soul!!

Bangle Seller
(चूड़ीहारिन)

Still remember that face
With a big black wart,
A bit hazy after
so long a Gap, yet not wiped out -
Even today I remember her face......
Full of love n Affection!!!!
Fondly known to all,
By the nickname -
'Bangle seller with a wart'.
Being the only
Bangle seller in whole
Village, she carried a
Big basket on her head,
Covered-properly with
A brown soiled sheet!!
'Take bangles, take bangles 'she would call out.
Even before she reached
From one to another lane, our
Grandmother sent someone to fetch her; She would come -
At once
Blinking her kohl- dyed eyes, breathing heavily;
With help, placing the basket down with a thud, Spread her
'Bhanumati ka pitara 'in
The court yard -
'Come..come..brides , newlyweds - come one and all. '
In very sweet jaggery-soaked tone, repeated
Her well known phrase,
I have'Selected these bangles

With much trouble ….'
Other than Multi coloured 'reshmi '
Bangles, sindoor, lac - bangles, tikuli, ribbons,
Pearl necklace, mirrors,
Nail polish and whatnots.
Cosmetics, displayed with much love n care and great Interest!
Colourful shining Bangles and
Delicate sahana lahthi Were put on wrists Lovingly, very slowly -
Saying, these are Married women's Grace.
Winning hearts with her
Sweet words, even cracking jokes …
She engaged everyone with -
Smiles, soft words gestures, twinkling eyes
And secretive gaze -
Narrating varied ins and outs of localities-They contributed to
Her marketing talent in selling off
Her products ….
'O my darlings! All are
Very solid …
Colours won't fade for months…with great pain
This time brought them from distant places….
Tales of people, surroundings,
Expert was she in selling her goods!
Said, sound of bangles announce, you are newlywed -
Alongwith she also took orders for next visit …
Lastly, calculations were done, money collected, kept in yellowed small purse, tuck on her waist..heaved a long sigh of relief .
We were amazed by her
Special love for our aunts and we sisters …Mother, aunties and all of us, sat around her
Until she satisfied all of us…

In hot summer noon
After much requests
She took only
A glass of sharbat…
Lifting her somewhat lighter basket
On her head,
Blessing and spraying love, warmth on all -
She went, promising
To come again.
Although, oflate,
Hardly any bangle - seller lady
Visits every house….
Yet
Yellow bangles in "Basant Panchami";
Green bangles in "Sawan", while red red Bangles in marriage season -
remind us of
Bangle selling lady,
Even in this machine age!!!

The lone Gulmohar
(एक अकेला गुलमोहर)

Entangled and scattered
I remained, but
Did not lose breath…
Complexities of life
In this way kept on
Improving….

Moon kept peeping
Through the window… Being the witness of your promises, kept setting.

Knots kept on forming
In thread of relationship
Moon - like night then
Kept on melting …

Wrapping the moon- light, I kept on weaving dreams …
Holding dews in hand
Kept washing my face ….

Your memories kept on
Raining ….
Lone Gulmohar kept on shedding leaves!!

I want to...
(जी चाहता है)

Seeing the rainbow Appear in the sky
I want to see myself
In those colours ....

The evenings when I met you everyday
Want to live once more
Those beautiful Evenings!

The memories which
Have no head or tail now
Want to keep them
Very carefully!!

The desires which could
Never be expressed
Want to narrate them
These days ...!!

Walking past you
Could smell a captivating
Scent ...
Want to become the
Touch of that scent ...!!

Devoted to your Name
(तेरे नाम पे निसार)

Can never forget the Time spent with you…Now I
Keep it alive with the
Manure of your Memories …

The moment I saw you,
Bloomed the garden of Mind …but
Now I just count those
Moments on my fingers !!…

How should I bury my
Feelings in heart…
I have just a tiny
Desperate heart…!!

They see a blooming
Garden in love …but
I see only dried withered
Flowers in old books!!

Your discussion creates
Music of 'Jal Trang' in
My ears …
Even today I am
Devoted to your Name...!!

Life with You
(ज़िंदगी तेरे साथ की)

Quietly sang the'ragini' of 'sitar' -
Of life imprisoned within margins!!

Dark night began to glimmer!!
Now that the vein of your Thought is opened ...!!

Like a musk deer, the
Footwear of your remembrance kept smelling with your
Own fragrance!!

Very quietly the scent of "Heena" is spreading ....
Eyes of the night of waiting have filled up!!

Life - like unsolved
Yellow documents...,
Many a time has Measured distances -
Of your thoughts!!!

Whenever the merciless
Thorns of Time
Grow on my thoughts,
Quietly remind me of
Life with you!!!

Why?
(क्यूँ)

Innocent
Was life's journey-
Injuring it why did you
Go away?

Drenching in the
Lively water falls of
Dreams, why did you go away?

Relaxed was I
With the style of your Conversing ….
Quietly, why did you
Go away?

Showering
Few drops of
Devotion through Love ...
Why did you go away?

Not even showed
The blooming garden…
Leaving heated-
Why did you go
Away?

Had lighted
Lamp of hope….
Dowsing it then
Why did you go away?

Maiika...
(मायका)

How straight and simple
Is the word,maiika…
Yes, "maiika", meaning -mother's home…
On hearing this word
Daughters are as
Overwhelmed as -
When a very poor man
Gets grains…or
Arrival of 'Basant'
After drought….
That's why
In the mind n soul
Of daughters,
Raw image of that home
Peeps lifelong!!

But maiika….
when mum is gone …

Mother, can you listen?
Yesterday only - every Lane of maiika was familiar... but today
Without you
Even the rooms of
Maiika are unfamiliar!!!

One - sided Love
(एकतरफ़ा मुहब्बत)

Interesting
Is one - sided love!!
It is that ROJA
Which has no IFTAR!!!

Wound of Heart
(दिल का ज़ख़्म)

There is no witness of
The
Wounds of heart!
And also
There is no court -session
For it!!

Questions
(सवाल)

It's not necessary that
We'll get answer to
All our questions!!
There are some
Questions that
Remain a Question
Forever!!!!

Love
(मोहब्बत)

LOVE is achieved
Not by Inheritance,
But by FATE;
And Fate cannot be
Written in
Testament!!!

Feelings
(एहसास)

When words
Are meaningless
And consolations
Purposeless; then
It is better to be silent
As
Feelings can't be forced
They come naturally
From within...

Night
(रात)

Night
Is always the same;
Only every time…
Each night
Has its own
Darkness.

That Time
(वो वक्त)

Whenever that time came,
For a moment…
Closing my eyes,
I talked with you!!
And
That difficult time
Was averted!!

The Age of Love
(मुहब्बत की उम्र)

Love is like
Human beings;
Some love weak;
Some small;
Some sick;
Some die in youth;
Some are even
A century old….
But-
Love certainly exists.

Unsuccessful Love
(नाकाम इश्क़)

In the Midstream -
Broken boat, defeated
Rudder…
Mute screams for life…
What can be a better
Picture of
Unsuccessful Love?

Alas
(काश)

So small a word is 'Alas '
But encompasses
A lot within …
When you ponder
Over it, you realise that
There's nothing before
God n his Creation.

Time
(वक्त)

Time has an answer
To every question
By hurrying up
We submerge ourselves
In more troubles !!)

Silence
(खामोशी)

Silence has
A tongue of its own;
Though it is inaudible
Upon reflection
It can be seen ….

Silence
(मौन)

Where the flight of stairs
Of words end
There's the roof
Of emotive silence -
No expression can ever
Explain it.

Life
(ज़िंदगी)

Sometimes I feel like
Beginning the Life
Once again
From that curve
Where both of us were
Strangers ....

Waiting
(इंतज़ार)

Sometimes as you
Keep waiting for Someone …
The habit to wait
Becomes so strong
That you begin
To like that habit!!

Winning
(जीत)

When human blood
Relationships
Are no more trustworthy,
The heart - beat in the
Chest
Also betrays…
That's why
Sometimes winning
Is more painful than
Losing….!!!!

Conversations
(गुफ्तगू)

Conversations just
Like windows,
Let in a breath of
Fresh air.
And lighten up the
Burden of heavy hearts
To a great extent!!!

Coincidence
(संयोग)

A strange coincidence
Is
That the day his memory
Becomes pain
And flows through the Eyes…
The jasmine tree
Planted by him…
Flowers-much more.

Relationship
(रिश्ता)

Every relationship
Denotes a hope;
Even if not Accomplished,
Teaches you
Something or the other.

Home
(घर)

If happiness could be
Purchased through
Homes built from
Engraved gems
Diamonds and marbles ...
Then "Taj Mahal. "
Would never be called
A Tomb.

A good sleep
(सुकून की नींद)

Very cheap are the
Sleeping pills!! But
Very precious
Is a peaceful good sleep;
It's not easy to get …
Many super Compromises
Have to be made!!!

9 788199 862500

Printed at Repro India Ltd.